STUMPED

(C   T)

by Shomit Dutta

‖SAMUEL FRENCH‖

Copyright © 2023 by Shomit Dutta
Cover artwork: Rebecca Pitt
All Rights Reserved

STUMPED is fully protected under the copyright laws of the British Commonwealth, including Canada, the United States of America, and all other countries of the Copyright Union. All rights, including professional and amateur stage productions, recitation, lecturing, public reading, motion picture, radio broadcasting, television, online/digital production, and the rights of translation into foreign languages are strictly reserved.

ISBN 978-0-573-01364-5

concordtheatricals.co.uk
concordtheatricals.com

FOR PRODUCTION ENQUIRIES

UNITED KINGDOM AND WORLD
EXCLUDING NORTH AMERICA
licensing@concordtheatricals.co.uk
020-7054-7298

NORTH AMERICA
info@concordtheatricals.com
1-866-979-0447

Each title is subject to availability from Concord Theatricals, depending upon country of performance.

CAUTION: Professional and amateur producers are hereby warned that *STUMPED* is subject to a licensing fee. The purchase, renting, lending or use of this book does not constitute a licence to perform this title(s), which licence must be obtained from the appropriate agent prior to any performance. Performance of this title(s) without a licence is a violation of copyright law and may subject the producer and/or presenter of such performances to penalties. Both amateurs and professionals considering a production are strongly advised to apply to the appropriate agent before starting rehearsals, advertising, or booking a theatre. A licensing fee must be paid whether the title is presented for charity or gain and whether or not admission is charged.

This work is published by Samuel French, an imprint of Concord Theatricals Ltd.

The Professional Rights in this play are controlled by Concord Theatricals, Aldwych House, 71-91 Aldwych, London, WC2B 4HN, UK.

No one shall make any changes in this title for the purpose of production. No part of this book may be reproduced, stored in a retrieval system, scanned, uploaded, or transmitted in any form, by any means, now known or yet to be invented, including mechanical, electronic, digital, photocopying, recording, videotaping, or otherwise, without the prior written permission of the publisher. No one shall share this title, or part of this title, to any social media or file hosting websites.

The moral right of Shomit Dutta to be identified as author of this work has been asserted in accordance with Section 77 of the Copyright, Designs and Patents Act 1988.

USE OF COPYRIGHTED MUSIC

A licence issued by Concord Theatricals to perform this play does not include permission to use the incidental music specified in this publication. In the United Kingdom: Where the place of performance is already licensed by the PERFORMING RIGHT SOCIETY (PRS) a return of the music used must be made to them. If the place of performance is not so licensed then application should be made to PRS for Music (www.prsformusic.com). A separate and additional licence from PHONOGRAPHIC PERFORMANCE LTD (www.ppluk.com) may be needed whenever commercial recordings are used. Outside the United Kingdom: Please contact the appropriate music licensing authority in your territory for the rights to any incidental music.

USE OF COPYRIGHTED THIRD-PARTY MATERIALS

Licensees are solely responsible for obtaining formal written permission from copyright owners to use copyrighted third-party materials (e.g., artworks, logos) in the performance of this play and are strongly cautioned to do so. If no such permission is obtained by the licensee, then the licensee must use only original materials that the licensee owns and controls. Licensees are solely responsible and liable for clearances of all third-party copyrighted materials, and shall indemnify the copyright owners of the play(s) and their licensing agent, Concord Theatricals Ltd., against any costs, expenses, losses and liabilities arising from the use of such copyrighted third-party materials by licensees.

IMPORTANT BILLING AND CREDIT REQUIREMENTS

If you have obtained performance rights to this title, please refer to your licensing agreement for important billing and credit requirements.

STUMPED was recorded as a digital 'On Demand' production by Original Theatre at Lords Cricket Ground, London, for release on 27th September 2022 with the following cast:

BECKETT .... Stephen Tompkinson
PINTER .... Andrew Lancel

STUMPED premiered as a live production, produced by Original Theatre, at the Theatre Royal Bath, 23rd May to 27th May 2023, the Cambridge Arts Theatre, 5th June to 10th June 2023, and Hampstead Theatre, 16th June to 22nd July 2023, with the following cast:

BECKETT .... Stephen Tompkinson
PINTER .... Andrew Lancel

Director | Guy Unsworth
David Woodhead | Set and Costume Designer
Howard Hudson | Lighting Designer
Dom Bilkley | Sound Designer
Mark Aspinall | Composer

The Irish premiere of *Stumped* will be at Bewley's Café Theatre, Dublin, 24th July to 19th August with the following cast:

BECKETT .... Barry McGovern
PINTER .... Michael James Ford

Director | Bairbre Ní Chaoimh

Original.

Operating and touring since 2004 the Original Theatre Company has toured extensively all over the UK and since 2020 have launched Original Theatre Online, producing a number of acclaimed online productions. In 2022, Original Theatre were awarded a Critics' Circle Theatre Award for our exceptional theatre-making during the Covid lockdowns.

Recent stage productions include: *The Time Machine*, *The Mirror Crack'd*, *The End of the Night* (a co-production with Park Theatre), *The Hound of the Baskervilles*, *Being Mr Wickham* (UK and New York), *A Splinter of Ice*, *The Croft*, Sarah Waters' *The Night Watch*, Stephen Jeffreys' *Valued Friends* (coproduction with Rose Theatre Kingston); Torben Betts' *Caroline's Kitchen* (originally Monogamy); Alan Bennett's *The Habit of Art* (UK & New York), Oscar Wilde's *The Importance of Being Earnest*, Frederick Knott's *Wait Until Dark*, Torben Betts' *Invincible*, Emlyn Williams' *Night Must Fall*, Terence Rattigan's *Flare Path* and the award winning tours of Sebastian Faulks's *Birdsong* adapted by Rachel Wagstaff.

FOR ORIGINAL THEATRE
Artistic Director | Alastair Whatley
Creative Producer | Tom Hackney
Show Producer | Joshua Beaumont
Digital Producer | Steven Atkinson
Head of Marketing | Emma Martin
Digital Theatre Manager | Thomas Moran
Production Co-ordinator | Lisa Friedrich
Social & Content | Paul Jennings for Hero Social
PR | Alison Duguid PR

www.originaltheatre.com
info@originaltheatre.com
@originaltheatre @originaltheatrecompany

ENTERTAINING WITH ORIGINALITY SINCE 1959

Hampstead Theatre was born in a humble hut sixty years ago, with a mission to produce original theatre without creative restriction. We quickly attracted a generation of talent that helped redefine British Theatre. From Harold Pinter testing out his early plays to the likes of Mike Leigh, Michael Frayn and Terry Johnson – and more recently Ruby Thomas, Nell Leyshon and Roy Williams, all premiering their work here.

Our home is one of London's best state-of-the-art theatres. Purpose built for the 21st century to allow our writers, actors, directors and producers maximum creative flexibility. Our ambitions are big as we aim to move theatre forwards with new ideas, talent and energy to excite our audiences with the lateral, the fresh and the unexpected. It's part of our belief that innovation, reinvention and surprise are the lifeblood of true entertainment.

Hampstead's beautiful Main Stage, with its epic dimensions and flexibility was built with directors and designers in mind. It has transported audiences into the 1924 Olympic Games amphitheatre (*Chariots of Fire*), to the intense traverse configuration of a courtroom (*55 Days*), deep into a Nottinghamshire coalmine (*Wonderland*) and on to the busy wards of an NHS hospital (*Tiger Country*).

Hampstead's Downstairs, is an intimate, 88-seat studio, established in 2012, since when it has been home to over 60 new plays. It is a much-loved space, wholly dedicated to new work, with a loyal following amongst audiences and artists alike. Through the Downstairs programme Hampstead continues to innovate and build on its exceptional foundations, as a theatre where new talent blossoms.

In 2023 Hampstead Theatre was delighted to welcome the brilliantly witty production of Shomit Dutta's *Stumped* to entertain our Downstairs audiences.

SUPPORTERS

Hampstead Theatre is grateful to its generous Patrons and Supporters, whose philanthropic underpinning ensures an outstanding calibre of creative work; highly subsidised ticket prices for young people, NHS and Emergency Services workers, seniors and people with access patrons and emerging playwright programmes.

RECENT ACCOLADES

Blackout Songs (Hampstead Downstairs) by Joe White, nominated for a 2023 Olivier Award for Outstanding Achievement in an Affiliate Theatre.

Rebecca Humphries wins a 2023 OffWestEnd Award for Best Lead Performance for *Blackout Songs*.

Ruby Thomas nominated for the 2023 Susan Smith Blackburn Prize for *Linck & Mülhahn*.

Folk (Hampstead Downstairs) by Nell Leyshon, nominated for a 2022 Olivier Award for Outstanding Achievement in an Affiliate Theatre.

Monique Touko wins Best Director for *Malindadzimu* (Hampstead Downstairs) at The Stage Debut Awards 2022.

The Phlebotomist (Hampstead Downstairs) by Ella Road, nominated for a 2019 Olivier Award for Outstanding Achievement in an Affiliate Theatre.

Ella Road nominated for the 2019 Susan Smith Blackburn Prize for *The Phlebotomist*.

Moe Bar-El nominated a 2019 Olivier Award for Best Actor for *Every Day I Make Greatness Happen* (Hampstead Downstairs).

Tony Kushner and Jeanine Tesori's *Caroline, or Change* nominated a 2019 Olivier Award for Best Musical Revival.

Sharon D. Clarke nominated for a 2019 Olivier Award for Best Actress in a Musical for *Caroline, or Change*.

Fly Davis nominated for a 2019 Olivier Award for Best Costume Design for *Caroline, or Change*.

CHARACTERS

BECKETT – a playwright, late 50s
PINTER – a playwright, mid 30s

SETTING

Oxfordshire.

TIME

Summer 1964.

AUTHOR'S NOTES

The idea for a play about Beckett and Pinter came about in the early 2000s. I was playing cricket for Gaieties CC (the club Pinter belonged to forty-odd years) and spending much of my time, as a D Phil student, unpicking the plays of Aristophanes. Some of these feature his favourite playwrights as characters, and my idea was to write an updated version of the *Frogs*, replacing Aeschylus and Euripides, who compete in the underworld for 'the Throne of Tragedy', with Beckett and Pinter. But for one reason or another it did not get written.

Some years later, in 2015, I helped organise a cricket match between a Pinter XI (Gaieties CC) and a Beckett XI (the Dublin-based Theatrical Cavaliers CC) for the 'Happy Days' Beckett festival in Enniskillen. It was suggested, rather last-minute, that as a complement to the game I write a comic skit involving Beckett and Pinter at a cricket match. I didn't want to do a rushed job so the play – now relocated from the underworld to the cricket field – remained unwritten.

In the spring of 2020, I found myself, along with everyone else, stuck in one place: finally, the ideal opportunity for writing the play. Moreover, The fact that Beckett and Pinter had also subjected their characters to enforced waiting in *Godot* and *The Dumb Waiter* created a conducive sense of *mise-en-abyme*.

I have always been interested in the relationship between a given author or text and other authors and texts (what academics dryly call intertextuality). Writing *Stumped* has allowed me to participate in this complex relationship creatively rather than simply observe it critically. I have also enjoyed subjecting two favourite authors to the exacting conditions that they impose on their hapless characters; in other words, giving them a dose of their own medicine.

Stumped exists in its original form and in a slightly longer one. The digital production and the forthcoming Irish premiere comprise the two main acts. The live production, in Bath and Cambridge ahead of a London run, includes a short third act or epilogue, written after the first lockdown. I'm not sure which I prefer. The play involves various 'twos'. There are two characters and two main acts, and there are two innings in the cricket match. At the same time, there are some 'threes': my original working title, *Yes... No... Wait*, refers to the three calls available to someone batting; and there are, including the epilogue, three acts. Perhaps it is fitting for a play where certainty proves elusive that the question of where it ought to end remains unresolved.

Shomit Dutta

ACT ONE

(A cricket ground in the Cotswolds, an overcast day in late June. Sounds of the game are heard throughout. The action takes place to one side of the pavilion. **BECKETT** *is seated on one of two folding chairs. He is padded up but has his coat on over his kit. He is watching the game and filling in a scorebook on his lap. Beside him a scoreboard reads twenty five for two off nine overs (and shows the first innings total of one hundred and seventy).* **PINTER** *is fetching his batting gear from the changing room.* **BECKETT** *has taken over the scoring to facilitate this.)*

(Throughout Act One **PINTER** *and* **BECKETT**, *though focused on the game, seem locked in a tacit duel where one inclines to direct confrontation while the other favours parry and surprise. Enter* **PINTER** *with his gear.)*

BECKETT. You could pad up.

PINTER. I am.

BECKETT. Is that a fact?

PINTER. I haven't finished yet.

BECKETT. You're in after me.

PINTER. I know.

(Pause. **BECKETT** *fills in the next ball (no run).* **PINTER** *sits but makes no effort to pad*

up. He is preoccupied with his boot and a bruise on his left ankle.)

BECKETT. Have you actually started?

PINTER. Yes.

BECKETT. In what respect?

PINTER. I'm wearing my box.

BECKETT. *(Aside.)* Mustn't neglect the little things...

(**BECKETT** *fills in the scorebook.*)

What's happening with our lift?

PINTER. We haven't even batted yet.

BECKETT. I like to have a secured exit.

PINTER. I've made some enquiries.

BECKETT. An old habit. *(Offhand.)* From my days in the French resistance.

PINTER. We're currently in the Cotswolds.

BECKETT. I'm aware of that.

(Pause. **BECKETT** *raises an arm to acknowledge a bye.)*

Our first run in two overs...

(**BECKETT** *fills in the scorebook.*)

PINTER. Are you planning to bat in that coat?

BECKETT. *(Thinking.)* I haven't ruled it out.

(**PINTER** *surveys* **BECKETT**'s *appearance.*)

PINTER. You seem... Somewhat out of sorts.

BECKETT. They're deep, my sorts. And I'm rarely out of them. But I am prone to superstition.

PINTER. I had no idea.

BECKETT. At least when it comes to batting.

PINTER. In that case, I'll redouble my efforts.

BECKETT. I'd prefer it if you added to your efforts, rather than multiplying.

PINTER. I'm not sure how to take that.

BECKETT. Perhaps in the spirit in which it was intended.

PINTER. Which was?

BECKETT. Strictly mathematical.

>   (**PINTER** *starts putting on his left pad. The lower strap proves painful. A cry of "Wait... Yes" from a batsman.*)

At last. A scoring shot.

(*Writing.*) Runs... one... Batsman...three.

>   (**PINTER** *starts to undo the pad.*)

PINTER. It's no good.

BECKETT. What?

PINTER. I have a swollen ankle.

BECKETT. A latter-day Oedipus.

PINTER. I acted in *Oedipus* as a young man.

BECKETT. Did your mama come?

PINTER. This was rural Ireland.

BECKETT. Beyond her clutch...

PINTER. I was playing Creon.

BECKETT. I see.

PINTER. Oedipus was fifty-six.

(*Beat.*)

BECKETT. Who played Jocasta? His fertile wife and mother.

PINTER. She was no spring chicken.

(**PINTER** *removes the pad and re-examines his ankle.* **BECKETT** *fills in the scorebook.*)

BECKETT. Does it hurt?

PINTER. (*Muttering.*) He wants to know if it hurts.

BECKETT. If you'd used your hand.

PINTER. My foot saved four runs.

BECKETT. The crack of leather on bone...

PINTER. Off your bowling.

BECKETT. The *sine qua non* of an English summer.

PINTER. (*Aside.*) He leaves no bone unpicked, no swelling lonely.

BECKETT. 'Heard by all the birds of Oxfordshire and Gloucestershire.'

PINTER. Am I pissing in the wind?

BECKETT. 'Adlestrop.'

(**BECKETT** *fills in the scorebook.*)

Twenty-seven for two off ten overs.

(**PINTER** *fiddles with the strap of his left pad.* **BECKETT** *gets up to update the scoreboard himself.*)

PINTER. This buckle could be more forgiving.

BECKETT. There's batsmen all over. Blaming on their pads the faults of their limbs.

(**PINTER** *removes his left boot and rests his injured foot on his right knee. He prods the injury. Meanwhile* **BECKETT** *raises an arm to acknowledge a leg bye.*)

PINTER. It needs ice.

(**BECKETT** *motions to rise.*)

BECKETT. I'll go.

PINTER. You can't.

BECKETT. Why not?

PINTER. You're doing the scorebook.

(**BECKETT** *sighs and resettles.*)

Besides, there's a notice: 'No spikes in the pavilion'.

(*As* **PINTER** *removes his other boot, a good ball whistles past the bat. We hear the fielders' "oohs".*)

BECKETT. (*Filling in the book.*) A dangerous bowler.

PINTER. What's this, his fifth over?

BECKETT. His sixth.

Hopefully, he won't have too many more.

(*They watch the next ball.*)

PINTER. I think I'll bat in tennis shoes.

BECKETT. A wise move.

PINTER. Kinder on the ankle.

BECKETT. It'll mean you can frequent the pavilion. (*Half-aside.*) Once you've padded up.

(**PINTER** *hobbles to the pavilion.* **BECKETT** *updates the book and briefly takes stock.*

(**PINTER** *returns with a bag of frozen vegetables and tennis shoes.*)

PINTER. Frozen peas. They need the ice for drinks.

BECKETT. Regular or petits pois?

(**PINTER** *puts down the tennis shoes and checks.*)

PINTER. Petits pois.

BECKETT. Smaller spheres. Better for the bruise.

PINTER. Is that so?

BECKETT. Though they will warm up faster.

(**PINTER** *starts applying his peas. Eleven overs are now complete and a new bowler is about to come on.*)

PINTER. A change of bowling.

BECKETT. Sadly at the wrong end. What's he called?

PINTER. *(Shouting out.)* Bowler's name?

(*A slightly unclear set of replies from the field.*)

BECKETT. What was that?

PINTER. ... Sergeant?

(**PINTER** *relays the nearest fielder's clarification.*)

Like the rank, but 'Sarge' with an 'a'.

(**BECKETT** *writes it in the book.*)

BECKETT. Let's hope he bowls some 'military medium'.

PINTER. Do you subscribe to nominative determinism?

BECKETT. Up to a point.

Named as I am, I avoid cathedrals.

> (**PINTER** *smiles. They watch the new bowler's first ball, which the batsman edges for a couple of streaky runs.*)

PINTER. Shot!

> (**BECKETT** *looks at* **PINTER** *askance. Cries from the field ("Yes" from the batsman followed by "Lucky bastard", "Save three", etc. from the fielders).*)

BECKETT. (*Writing.*) Runs... two... Batsman... four.

> (*Pause. They watch the next ball.*)

How's your filmscript going?

> (**PINTER** *has to think.*)

The three-way project with Ionesco.

PINTER. To be honest, it's somewhat dormant.

BECKETT. (*Eying the pads.*) Like your efforts here...

PINTER. I have a working title. 'The Compartment'.

> (*No response.*)

It bears a resemblance to your latest play.

BECKETT. In what respect?

PINTER. It's a *ménage à trois*. What was it called, again?

BECKETT. (*Filling in the scorebook.*) 'Play'.

PINTER. Although where you have a man and two women, I have a woman and two men.

BECKETT. Are any of them housed in jars?

PINTER. No. The similarity ends there.

(**BECKETT** *raises his arm to acknowledge a leg bye.*)

BECKETT. *(Totting them up.)* Our... ninth leg bye.

PINTER. What about *your* filmscript?

BECKETT. Finished some time ago.

PINTER. What's it called, again?

BECKETT. *'Film'*. They start on it next month.

(**PINTER** *digests this.* **BECKETT** *fills in the scorebook.*)

PINTER. Did you get Chaplin?

BECKETT. Buster Keaton.

PINTER. Not bad...

BECKETT. I doubt he's read it.

PINTER. That's film actors for you. Leave everything till the last minute.

BECKETT. I believe you've acted in some films yourself.

(Beat.)

PINTER. I'll return to *'The Compartment'* as soon as I can. Though I should warn you. I'm getting my teeth into a new play.

BECKETT. *(Filling in the scorebook.)* Thirty-one for two off twelve.

PINTER. Perhaps you're wondering what it's about?

BECKETT. *(Offhand.)* Not really.

(**PINTER** *looks slightly grazed.*)

When are our plays about anything?

PINTER. You speak of our work in tandem.

(**BECKETT** *gets up to update the scoreboard.*)

BECKETT. Our methods are very different.

PINTER. Shall I tell you who's in it?

BECKETT. They both involve wounds,

PINTER. There's a retired butcher,

BECKETT. Festering, leprous,

PINTER. Left by his wife.

BECKETT. Weeping, putrescent.

PINTER. She died years ago.

BECKETT. But with my characters,

PINTER. He lives with his brother,

BECKETT. The wounds are exposed,

PINTER. A jobbing chauffeur,

BECKETT. The outlook is hopeless,

PINTER. And two of his sons.

BECKETT. And yet they press on…

PINTER. Neither does much.

BECKETT. …*ad nauseam.*

(**BECKETT** *sits and starts updating the scorebook.*)

PINTER. The third's an academic.

BECKETT. Your characters are different.

PINTER. He visits from America,

BECKETT. The wounds are concealed,

PINTER. With his shadowy wife.

BECKETT. Fiercely contained,

PINTER. The thing's set in London.

BECKETT. Till slowly but surely,

PINTER. I have a strange feeling

BECKETT. They come to a head.

PINTER. She'll stir things up.

> (*A cry of "Wait... Yes" from the field.*)

No title as yet.

BECKETT. (*About to write.*) Runs... one... Batsman...

> (**BECKETT** *looks up from the book to the two batsmen.*)

Which of these players is which?

PINTER. This end is (*Peering.*) ... Fred Paolozzi.

BECKETT. (*Checking.*) That's a relief.

PINTER. Fred's a flyman at the Palladium.

BECKETT. (*Filling it in.*) In terms of the scorebook.

PINTER. He also coaches at the Gover school of cricket. It's through him that I got involved with the club. He has a wonderful eye. Can hit the ball miles.

BECKETT. But not today.

PINTER. The other end is 'Young Dick Wyse'.

BECKETT. (*Looking in the scorebook.*) Number four.

PINTER. At least, that's what they call him. Joined just before me. I think he's a medical student.

BECKETT. So neither is the man who might give us a lift?

> (*A cry of 'no-ball' from the umpire.* **BECKETT** *raises a hand to acknowledge.*)

PINTER. Fred's probably going back with the skipper.

BECKETT. The skipper...

    (**BECKETT** *looks for him in the scorebook.*)

PINTER. Laurie Lupino-Lane.

BECKETT. *(Still looking.)* Batting at...

PINTER. Son of *Lupino* Lane.

BECKETT. ...number nine.

PINTER. The music hall star, who set up the club.

I found out earlier that Laurie's just taken on a dwarf who used to perform with his father, as his butler.

BECKETT. *(Filling in the scorebook.)* Is that so?

PINTER. Apparently he's less than three feet tall.

BECKETT. What about Dick Wyse?

PINTER. I doubt he has a butler.

BECKETT. Does he drive?

PINTER. When I spoke to Laurie about a lift back to London, he said this other chap was our best bet.

BECKETT. What 'other chap'?

PINTER. Our putative driver.

BECKETT. What's he called?

PINTER. I've no idea.

BECKETT. *(Scanning the book.)* Must be one of these.

PINTER. It stands to reason.

BECKETT. *(Still looking.)* Though there is the odd gap in the batting order.

PINTER. Laurie said he'd ask him on our behalf.

BECKETT. Has that happened yet?

PINTER. I'm not sure.

BECKETT. But you know him by sight?

PINTER. *(Gingerly.)* Not as such.

> (**BECKETT** *sighs in frustration.*)

Still, we must have seen him. Assuming he's playing.

BECKETT. Can we at least give him a name?

For morale, if nothing else.

PINTER. Do you have one in mind?

BECKETT. What about… Doggo?

PINTER. Doggo?

BECKETT. A reflection of his attitude.

PINTER. As in '*lying* doggo'?

BECKETT. He's eluded us thus far.

> (**PINTER** *carries on icing his bruise.* **BECKETT** *glances at him periodically with growing irritation.*)

(Filling in the book.) Two off the over… Thirty-three for two off thirteen.

> *(The situation continues.)*

Can you not pad up before applying those bloody peas?

PINTER. They're not peas… they're petits / pois.

BECKETT. *(Erupting.)* Just put on the fucking pads!

> *(Tension.* **BECKETT** *gets up and starts pacing about.)*

PINTER. Why are you getting so exercised?

(**BECKETT** *stops to update the scoreboard (thirty three for two off thirteen overs), tendering his explanation as he does so.*)

BECKETT. We were always taught at school that the next two batsmen should be padded up. If you, as the man in after me, decline to pad up, I fear that...

PINTER. What?

BECKETT. That fate may deem it an act of hubris and see *me* sent in quickly and swiftly dismissed, as prologue to *your* comeuppance.

PINTER. (*Digesting this.*) If I'd realised the gravity of your condition, I'd have acted sooner.

(**BECKETT** *sits back down and takes a deep breath.*)

BECKETT. Batsmen are especially prone to such things. I remember some in the Portora first eleven who, on the day of a game, avoided shaving, smoking, even masturbating.

PINTER. I don't envy you or your schooling.

Still, I suppose, it's in keeping with your nature.

BECKETT. Masturbating?

PINTER. Agonising first and acting later.

BECKETT. As opposed to acting at leisure and repenting in haste?

(*Pause.* **BECKETT** *takes up the scorebook and pen.*)

I missed the last two balls.

PINTER. Both dots.

BECKETT. No...

(**BECKETT** *looks from field to scorebook to field again.*)

Paolozzi must have got a single.

(**BECKETT** *updates the book.* **PINTER** *observes him.*)

PINTER. I could throw you a few in the nets.

BECKETT. No.

PINTER. Once I've padded up.

BECKETT. My first innings in thirty-five years. I'd rather not be reminded of my decrepitude.

PINTER. You're hardly decrepit.

BECKETT. Pad up promptly, and we may yet placate the umpire in the sky. Assuming he's open to appeasing.

PINTER. Or appealing...

(**PINTER** *puts on his tennis shoes, and sighs deeply.*)

BECKETT. (*Noticing.*) 'For this relief much thanks.'

PINTER. *Hamlet.*

BECKETT. Act one, scene one.

PINTER. Line eight. Francisco to Barnardo.

(**BECKETT** *eyes him.*)

I was in *Hamlet* as well.

BECKETT. You don't say.

(*Filling in the scorebook.*) Let me guess... Ophelia.

PINTER. Horatio. I understudied Hamlet.

BECKETT. Was this also in Ireland?

PINTER. I got to play him once. A one-off matinee in a convent. Our regular lead –

BECKETT. Not the man who played Oedipus?

PINTER. How did you guess?

BECKETT. A stab in the dark…

PINTER. Mac, our seasoned Danish prince, was laid low by a cold and a hangover from hell. So on I went. Perhaps the only actor to have uttered the line, 'Get thee to a nunnery', in a nunnery.

BECKETT. How did it go down?

PINTER. Limply.

BECKETT. Not with a bang but a wimple…

    (**PINTER** *eyes him.*)

Just thinking aloud. What did Mac say?

PINTER. *(Irish accent.)* 'Not bad. Next time be kinder to your mother'.

    (**BECKETT** *laughs. They watch the next ball in silence.*)

I need a cup of tea. Shall I get you one?

BECKETT. I'd prefer something stronger.

PINTER. *(Getting up.)* I'll see if the bar's open.

BECKETT. *(Pleadingly.)* Will you not pad up first?

PINTER. As soon as I've got my tea.

    (**PINTER** *starts hobbling off towards the pavilion.*)

BECKETT. What time is it?

PINTER. *(Checking his watch.)* Five-ish.

BECKETT. Is the minute hand over the yardarm?

PINTER. Why?

BECKETT. I never drink beer before five, or tea after.

PINTER. Is that a strict rule?

BECKETT. *(Concessive.)* One more honoured in the breach than the observance.

> (**PINTER** *wryly notes the reference and limps off to the pavilion.* **BECKETT** *updates the scorebook.* **PINTER** *reappears shortly afterwards.*)

PINTER. The bar opens at five. It's three minutes to. I can go in and wait.

BECKETT. No, I'll stick with tea for now.

> (**BECKETT** *raises an arm to acknowledge a signal.*)

PINTER. As it comes?

BECKETT. I assume it comes with milk.

PINTER. I was thinking of sugar.

BECKETT. Sugar is a must.

PINTER. How much?

BECKETT. Three.

PINTER. Spoons?

BECKETT. What else would they have?

PINTER. Cubes? Lumps?

BECKETT. Lumps?

PINTER. It's possible.

BECKETT. *(Filling in the scorebook.)* How big?

PINTER. I've no idea.

BECKETT. I'll leave it to you. Only don't be long.

(**PINTER** *goes back to the pavilion.* **BECKETT** *updates the scoreboard (thirty-five for two off fourteen overs) and sits back down.* **PINTER** *returns and gives* **BECKETT** *his tea.*)

PINTER. The lumps were large. I put in two and brought a third in case.

(**PINTER** *hands* **BECKETT** *a lump of sugar.* **BECKETT** *examines it, puts it in, and has a tiny sip.*)

BECKETT. Ugh!

PINTER. Too sweet?

BECKETT. Too strong.

(**BECKETT** *takes another tentative sip.*)

This isn't tea, it's gravy. Is the bag still in there?

PINTER. It was straight from the pot.

BECKETT. Perhaps one escaped, and stewed there.

PINTER. How?

BECKETT. Was it a generous spout?

PINTER. Not that I recall. The pot was fairly empty. They relit it on the gas.

BECKETT. They lit the pot?

PINTER. It was stainless steel. I'll get you a spoon.

BECKETT. Wait,

(**PINTER** *heads back in.* **BECKETT** *fills in the scorebook.* **PINTER** *returns with a spoon and a plate of biscuits.*)

PINTER. Here you go. Biscuits to boot.

BECKETT. What class?

PINTER. Digestives.

BECKETT. Brand?

PINTER. *(Doggedly.)* McVities.

> (**PINTER** *puts down the plate and hands* **BECKETT** *the spoon.* **BECKETT** *dips it in. Fishing around briefly, he produces a tea bag.)*

BECKETT. Ah! The little rascal.

> *(He deposits the teabag on the side of the biscuit plate and takes another sip of tea with a mild grimace.)*

PINTER. When did you last play cricket?

BECKETT. *(Thinking.)* Nineteen... twenty-eight.

PINTER. Before I was born.

> *(They absorb this.* **BECKETT** *fills in the scorebook.)*

BECKETT. You? Before joining this lot?

> (**PINTER** *starts to contemplate the question but is suddenly startled.)*

PINTER. Something just landed in my tea!

BECKETT. Flower or beast?

PINTER. *(Looking.)* An insect of some kind.

BECKETT. A wasp?

PINTER. Looks more like a hornet.

BECKETT. Is it dead?

PINTER. It soon will be. Boiled alive.

BECKETT. *(Aside.)* In a Dantean pool of molten fire.

PINTER. It's still flailing!

> *(A call of 'yes' from the field, as **PINTER** tries to extract the creature. **BECKETT** fills in the book.)*

BECKETT. Runs two... Batsman...

PINTER. Aaggh!

BECKETT. You've been bitten!

PINTER. Burnt! This tea's scorching.

> *(**PINTER** examines his fingers.)*

PINTER. Pass me your spoon.

BECKETT. To save it?

PINTER. Yes...

> *(**BECKETT** is on the point of passing him the spoon.)*

No, wait, I'll crush it,

BECKETT. *(Refusing to let go.)* No!

> *(They tussle. The scorebook falls off **BECKETT**'s lap.)*

PINTER. Squash it against the side.

BECKETT. I won't connive in such savagery.

> *(**BECKETT** uses a feint so that **PINTER** can lean on his foot.)*

PINTER. *(Wincing.)* Aahh!

> *(**BECKETT** wins the spoon and gets the scorebook.)*

(Grudgingly.) Fine.

> (**PINTER** *covers his cup with the biscuit plate.*)

We'll leave it to its fate.

BECKETT. It'll come back to bite you.

PINTER. Hornets don't bite,

BECKETT. Like Oedipus.

PINTER. They prick.

> (**BECKETT** *stands with the scorebook.* **PINTER** *remains seated. They watch the next ball.* **PINTER** *winces.*)

Wyse is going to nick one soon.

BECKETT. For the love of Mike, put on those pads.

> (**PINTER** *finally complies.* **BECKETT** *starts pacing back and forth checking on his progress.*)

PINTER. Would you mind sitting down?

BECKETT. What does my attitude matter?

PINTER. I'm not doing this with you stalking up and down like John Gabriel Borkman.

> (**BECKETT** *sits. He examines a biscuit.*)

BECKETT. I can't eat these without a serviceable drink.

> (*No response.* **PINTER** *continues padding up slowly, as* **BECKETT** *fills in the scorebook.*)

Thirty-seven for two off fifteen.

> (**BECKETT** *looks impatiently at* **PINTER**.)

Can you not do the scoreboard? Just this once?

PINTER. I'm padding up.

(**BECKETT** *sighs then gets up and does it. As he sits back down, a bell rings from inside the pavilion.*)

BECKETT. What's that?

PINTER. The bar!

BECKETT. We're saved!

(*They look at each other.*)

(*Rising.*) I'll go.

PINTER. You can't.

BECKETT. Why not?

PINTER. You'll tear up the carpet.

(**BECKETT** *sighs and resettles.*)

I'm almost done… There!

(**PINTER** *is finally padded up.*)

BECKETT. (*Viscerally relieved.*) At, bloody, last!

(**PINTER** *gets up to go to the bar.*)

PINTER. What'll you have?

BECKETT. What do they peddle in these parts? Porter?

PINTER. I doubt it.

BECKETT. Plain?

PINTER. 'A pint of plain is sadly not your man'.

BECKETT. They do have beer?

PINTER. I'm told there's a passable local bitter.

BECKETT. Then let's drink it, and pass it. A little *courage Hollandais* before entering the fray.

> (**PINTER** *goes in to the bar.* **BECKETT** *watches the next twos balls. He is looking down, filling in the scorebook, as* **PINTER** *returns with drinks.*)

PINTER. A wicket!

BECKETT. *(Jumping up.)* What?!

> (**BECKETT** *drops the pen and scorebook, and starts looking for his bat and gloves.*)

PINTER. In the test.

BECKETT. Jesus wept!

> (**BECKETT** *sits back up and sighs with relief.*)

PINTER. England are batting.

BECKETT. I thought I was in for a minute.

PINTER. There's a radio behind the bar.

> (**BECKETT** *retrieves the scorebook and pen.* **PINTER** *gives* **BECKETT** *his beer. Calm is restored.*)

You seemed positively alarmed.

BECKETT. Chiefly at the prospect of going out unfortified.

PINTER. Well, here's to two fruitful innings!

BECKETT. May Flora and Pomona smile on our efforts!

> (*They clink glasses and drink.* **BECKETT** *puts his drink down and updates the scorebook.*)

Who's out at Lords? Not Edrich?

PINTER. No. Phil Sharpe.

BECKETT. The slip fielder extraordinaire...

PINTER. I think they're five down.

BECKETT. Who's in next?

PINTER. Jim Parks.

(BECKETT has to think for a moment.)

The Sussex keeper.

BECKETT. Ah, yes.

PINTER. A useful batsman. His father played one test.

BECKETT. You're a mine of information.

PINTER. I have a few volumes of Wisden at home. Including one that features you.

(BECKETT looks at him askance.)

Trinity versus Northants, nineteen twenty-five.

BECKETT. Oh, that... A washout, if memory serves.

PINTER. You scored eighteen and twelve in the university's two innings.

BECKETT. *(Filling in the scorebook.)* I was mopped up in the first innings by a bowler called Towell.

PINTER. Northamptonshire only had one innings, in which you bowled eight overs, including two maidens, and took no wicket for seventeen.

BECKETT. A frugal spell, albeit unfruitful.

You seem to know the scorecard well.

(No reply. They watch the next ball...)

PINTER. Shot!

BECKETT. Our first boundary. *(Filling in the scorebook.)* Forty-one for two... off sixteen.

PINTER. I'll put it up.

> (**PINTER** *updates the scoreboard.* **BECKETT** *is warmed by* **PINTER***'s cooperative gesture.*)

BECKETT. I have, on occasion, thought of Vladimir and Estragon as a pair of England batsmen. Numbers five and six. *(Pointing to the two of them.)* Padded up and waiting to go in.

PINTER. Mood?

BECKETT. Fretful.

PINTER. Weather?

BECKETT. Overcast.

PINTER. Temperature?

BECKETT. Indifferent.

PINTER. Format of the game?

BECKETT. A timeless test.

PINTER. Location?

BECKETT. Lords.

PINTER. Where the field is full of shades,

BECKETT. As they near the shadowy coast.

PINTER. Will they ever reach it?

BECKETT. I very much doubt it.

PINTER. Oh my Didi and my Gogo, long ago...

BECKETT. They must remain forever trapped... Leg before wicket... In no man's land.

PINTER. That's very good.

> (*Pause.* **BECKETT** *fills in the scorebook. They watch the next ball in silence.* **PINTER** *lights a cigarette.*)

You'll never guess who one of the umpires is - in the test.

BECKETT. I'm not up on my match officials.

PINTER. Jack Crapp.

BECKETT. Get away! Is that with a 'C' or a 'K'?

PINTER. The commentators neglected to spell it.

BECKETT. Ignorant apes.

PINTER. I think it's a 'C', and a double 'P'.

> *(Something happens on the pitch (various 'Howzats').)*

What was that?

BECKETT. *(Startled.)* Where?!

PINTER. Is he out?

BECKETT. Christ...

PINTER. I think you're in.

> *(**BECKETT**, dazed and flustered, passes the scorebook, picks up his bat and gloves, and starts heading out.)*

Sam! *(**BECKETT** turns.)* Your coat...

> *(**BECKETT** returns and removes his coat. **PINTER** holds his gloves and bat for him while he does so, then returns them. **BECKETT** turns and starts to go out again, but stops.)*

BECKETT. I can't do this.

PINTER. *(Hands on his shoulders.)* Yes, you can. You're a far better player, a far better man, than I'll ever be.

BECKETT. I'm not sure you're right on either score.

(**PINTER** *reflects on this.* **BECKETT** *gathers himself.*)

Old Phil Sharpe, how was he out?

PINTER. *(Thinking.)* Leg before wicket.

BECKETT. A Crapp decision?

PINTER. Very possibly.

BECKETT. Let's hope I don't get one of those out there.

(**BECKETT** *drains his glass before walking out to bat.*)

Slow Fade

ACT TWO

(Midnight, somewhere nearby. Moonlight. Sound of nightbirds. Enter **PINTER** *with his bag, still limping but less aware of it. He emerges from woods (offstage right) onto a green open space. He puts down his bag (downstage) and looks around to see where they are.)*

PINTER. *(To himself.)* Utterly arseholed.

(He goes back to where he entered.)

(To **BECKETT**.*)* Hurry up!

BECKETT. *(Offstage.)* I'm coming.

PINTER. Are you even moving?

BECKETT. *(Offstage.)* No, but my waters are.

I'm imagining what it is to be a rain god.

PINTER. *(To himself.)* You and your fucking gods!

BECKETT. *(Offstage.)* Except where Jupiter unleashed a mighty torrent, I tease out a meagre dribble.

PINTER. Dribble any longer, we'll miss the boat.

*(***PINTER*** heads back to his bag. Enter* **BECKETT***, his head bandaged, holding his bag.)*

BECKETT. What boat?

PINTER. Our passage back.

BECKETT. My front passage was a more pressing concern.

> (**BECKETT** *does up his flies and puts down his bag.* **PINTER** *assesses his state and appearance.*)

PINTER. You don't look like a weather god. Not with that bandage on your head.

BECKETT. They say Jupiter gave birth to Minerva through a gash in his head, made by Vulcan's axe. Just as you banjaxed me with your bat.

PINTER. I didn't hit you with my bat.

BECKETT. You used a ball to drive home your point.

PINTER. What did you give birth to?

BECKETT. It was more like a death. Hard and bitter.

> (*He picks up his bag and looks out into the darkness.*)

Let's go?

PINTER. We're here.

BECKETT. Where?

PINTER. The village green.

BECKETT. (*Looking around.*) Are you sure?

PINTER. Nowhere has two village greens.

BECKETT. I was wondering if this qualifies.

PINTER. It's green. A village lies beyond.

> (*He scans the relevant horizon and puts down his bags.*)

BECKETT. What now?

PINTER. We wait. Assuming our lift hasn't been and gone.

BECKETT. And that we're in the right place.

(**BECKETT** *sits on the ground and leans back, legs outstretched.*)

potus... ut eruptio.

PINTER. English?

BECKETT. Pissed as a fart.

PINTER. I'm several sheets to the wind myself.

BECKETT. Though your average Roman would baulk at such an infelicitous comparison.

PINTER. What would he have said?

BECKETT. *potus ut piscis*?

PINTER. Pissed as a kiss?

BECKETT. Drunk as a fish.

Either way, I'm totally plastered.

PINTER. Back to Anglo-Saxon...

BECKETT. From *membrum* to beak.

PINTER. With the odd lapse.

BECKETT. The tendency to Latinise is hard to break.

PINTER. A testament to your upright schooling.

BECKETT. I'm hardly upright now. *homo dejectus*, rarely *erectus*. How are you bearing up?

PINTER. I'm galled, sore-footed...

(*Sighing deep.*) I can't believe I fucked up the game.

(**BECKETT** *laughs involuntarily.*)

BECKETT. It certainly was a shambles. Still, you mustn't blame yourself. I was flagging anyway.

PINTER. You were destined for a fifty. It was my fault that our batting collapsed, and we were bowled out for ninety.

> (**PINTER** *puts his head in his hands and groans in despair.*)

BECKETT. You shouldn't be so hard on yourself. You weren't the author of our downfall.

PINTER. Its agent...

BECKETT. Agency requires autonomy. In your case there was none.

PINTER. I was a curse.

BECKETT. You were a poor player. Following a script penned from on high. Who strutted and fretted his minute at the crease and then, thankfully, was seen no more.

PINTER. I was an idiot full of sound and fury, achieving bugger all.

BECKETT. It was an invidious part, I grant you. Yet in purely dramatic terms, it was a plumb role. And you played it with aplomb. Like Richard the Third. Or Edmund the Bastard.

PINTER. All I wanted was not to get out first ball. That's what happened last week. My debut for the club. I hit a glorious straight drive, smack in the middle of the bat... And the bowler caught it.

BECKETT. Hah!

PINTER. Christ, I need a drink...

> (**PINTER** *goes to his bag and gets a half-full bottle of whisky, along with two receptacles. He pours them drinks, hands* **BECKETT** *his, and sits down.*)

For God's sake, let us sit upon the green and tell sad stories of the fall of batsmen.

And we should start with you.

(Raising his glass.) I've never seen a more sublime eighteen.

BECKETT. Get away.

PINTER. A miniature masterpiece!

BECKETT. You're too fulsome.

PINTER. A perfect range of stroke and execution.

BECKETT. You see it through the rosy tint of booze and remorse.

PINTER. I remember it all. *(Simulating shots.)* The checked pull shot and flashing cover drive for four. The firm push for three between bowler and stumps. The two twos, guided through point and clipped through midwicket. Even the singles. The nurdle past gully, the steer into the covers and that deft leg glance.

*(**BECKETT** is struck by **PINTER**'s detailed memory.)*

It was a dream start to what would have been a match-winning innings. Then I came in…

*(**PINTER** clutches his head in his hands again.)*

BECKETT. Stop flailing yourself. Any fluency came from a total lack of expectation. As soon as I had hopes, I was doomed.

PINTER. You're just humouring me.

BECKETT. Not at all.

*(**PINTER** starts to unfurl.)*

Let's review your innings…

PINTER. Let's not.

BECKETT. It was short compared with mine. Yet it would have been better if it were shorter still. It puts me in mind of what the Greeks called –

PINTER. Those bloody Greeks!

BECKETT. …the wisdom of Silenus.

PINTER. Who the fuck was he?

BECKETT. The bosom pal of Bacchus. A sort of ancient Falstaff.

PINTER. Is there a limerick about him?

BECKETT. No.

PINTER. There was an old man called Silenus,

Endowed with / an oversized…

BECKETT. Stop it!

PINTER. *(Sitting up.)* What did he have to say, this chummy-bum of Bacchus?

BECKETT. 'Best never to have been born at all; second best to die as soon as possible.'

PINTER. Your worldview in a nutshell…

BECKETT. Birth *is* the meat of the problem.

PINTER. Perhaps we should style you 'the lean Silenus'.

BECKETT. Your innings was a whirlwind affair. Just three balls to my twenty-odd. And yet it was richer in incident, deeper in consequence, broader in generic coloration. There were shades of comedy, tragedy, melodrama, burlesque, slapstick, pantomime, theatre of the absurd, theatre of cruelty, vaudeville, *commedia del arte* and, last but not least, farce.

PINTER. Are we done?

BECKETT. That was just the prologue.

PINTER. Christ on a bike!

BECKETT. *(Warming to his theme.)* Your first ball you hoisted for six, off neither front foot nor back. I was still digesting it, when you creamed the next ball, a high full toss, back down the pitch and struck me on the head. The ball ricocheted off my dented skull to the man at mid-on, who caught it. The fielding side appealed, but the umpire called, 'no ball'. I might have survived but on hearing you say 'wait' I lurched forward and came to ground *out* of my ground.

PINTER. I did say 'no'.

BECKETT. You also said 'yes'.

PINTER. The messages were mixed...

BECKETT. The fielder in question, realising that the catch didn't count, threw down the stumps at the bowler's end. I remained oblivious throughout.

> (**PINTER** *clutches his head and curls up again.*)

I go through it not to shame you, but as an act of redemption.

PINTER. They lacked the decency to retract the appeal. Couldn't risk you retiring hurt and coming back in to win the game.

BECKETT. The new batsman was our number seven.

PINTER. Please don't go on.

BECKETT. I'm only a third of the way through your innings. The next delivery I'm told you attempted a swipe-to-leg, which spooned off the toe of the bat into the off-side.

PINTER. I played too early.

BECKETT. Shaken, perhaps, by my violent demise.

As I understand it, you called your new partner through for a single. To his cost, he responded - little knowing you would buckle the instant you leant on your wounded ankle.

PINTER. I tried to send him back.

BECKETT. He was left stranded, halfway down the pitch. Run out by ten yards. without even facing a ball. The precise sequence of your calling - correct me if I'm wrong - was 'Yes... No... Wait'.

Why the 'Wait'? After the 'No'. What did it add?

PINTER. I just...

BECKETT. As it was, the fielder swanned up to the stumps with the ball and flicked off the bails. Number seven stormed back to the pavilion, cursing you to high heaven and put his bat through a window. He said he'd never heard such abysmal calling in all his life.

> (*No response.* **PINTER** *slowly starts to look up.*)

The next ball,

PINTER. Must you go on?

BECKETT. I must. And you must hear it.

PINTER. You're enjoying this.

BECKETT. (*Serenely.*) Not at all.

The next ball, technically your third, on account of the earlier no-ball, you were clean bowled by a delivery that you claim swang both ways in the air.

PINTER. (*Feebly.*) It did.

(**PINTER** *looks blank.* **BECKETT** *tops up their glasses.*)

BECKETT. *(Raising his glass.)* To the miserable man who batted at seven. *(To himself.)* I say 'batted' …

PINTER. I know nothing about him. Except that he was our best player but the skipper had asked him to drop down the order so that we would get a chance to bat.

BECKETT. I hope he didn't have to travel far.

(No response.)

Strangely enough, he was my age but your build.

(Beat.)

He could have been your father.

PINTER. My father's very short.

BECKETT. Mine wasn't…

(**BECKETT** *begins to move downstage. As he does, he becomes uncharacteristically unguarded, speaking more into the darkness than to* **PINTER** *as such.*)

We used to go for walks in the Wicklow mountains… Long, often silent affairs… Unmarred by the vulgarity of speech… Rock and heath, grassland and bog.

(He thinks for a moment about a lost loved one who died in the same year as his father.)

Man alive, is that a gibbet?

PINTER. Where?

(He locates it. They both continue to look out.)

Would they have executed people on the village green?

BECKETT. I wouldn't put it past them. This *is* England.

(*Beat.*)

PINTER. That's where our number seven would like to see me rot.

BECKETT. A fitting end for both of us.

PINTER. Why you?

BECKETT. I was born on Friday the thirteenth of April. Not just Friday the thirteenth but Good Friday.

No one comes back from that.

PINTER. Except Jesus.

(*Pause.*)

I've just realised.

BECKETT. What?

PINTER. We never worked out Doggo's actual name.

BECKETT. We didn't put a face to him either.

(**BECKETT** *starts to look unsettled.*)

PINTER. What's wrong?

BECKETT. I'm having doubts.

PINTER. What about?

BECKETT. The arrangement.

PINTER. I thought you only agonised beforehand.

BECKETT. This was *your* arrangement.

PINTER. The message was clear.

BECKETT. From the skipper?

PINTER. Well, actually, it was one of the others. But he had it on good authority from the skipper. Who had it straight from Doggo himself. To wait on the village green between closing time and twelve. By the willow tree…

BECKETT. Why was it not discussed with Doggo in person?

PINTER. He left before the end of the game. To visit his aunt. He was meant to be going for lunch, but moved lunch to dinner because we were one short.

BECKETT. Is this nearby?

PINTER. Somewhere between… Upper Slaughter… Lower Swell and… Oddington.

BECKETT. I'm none the wiser.

PINTER. Not far from Adlestrop.

BECKETT. Adlestrop?

PINTER. Just north of here. On the branch line to Oxford.

(BECKETT thinks.)

BECKETT. I read somewhere that Edward Thomas took the train journey described in 'Adlestrop' in 1914. 'It was late June', the poem says. It could have been fifty years ago to the day. 'No one left and no one came / on the bare platform'.

It's stayed with me that line.

(Beat.)

PINTER. Let's find this tree.

(They advance to the edge of the stage and look out.)

Probably this one. It looks like a willow.

BECKETT. Willow or ash?

PINTER. What do you mean? You think it's the wrong tree?

BECKETT. Not necessarily.

PINTER. Neither of us are poets of nature.

BECKETT. I'm grazed by that assertion.

PINTER. You explore dystopias. I've only set one play outdoors.

> *(Pause. They both take a moment to reflect on their situation.)*

BECKETT. What did he do in the game?

PINTER. Doggo?

BECKETT. We've established he was playing. What did he do? Did he bowl?

PINTER. I don't think so.

> *(**BECKETT** suddenly goes to check his bag.)*

We only used, what, four bowlers?

BECKETT. *(Abruptly.)* Oh God!

PINTER. What?

BECKETT. I've left my coat.

PINTER. In the wood?

BECKETT. At the ground.

> *(**PINTER** thinks. **BECKETT** puts his head in his hands.)*

PINTER. We can't go back now. We wouldn't find our way.

BECKETT. That coat was my shield,

PINTER. We'll have to ring in the morning.

BECKETT. My tattered arras against the ingress of cold and egress of malodour.

PINTER. I've got a spare jumper.

BECKETT. *(Looking up.)* No. I'll soldier on.

PINTER. *(Sincerely.)* You have my deepest sympathies.

(Pause.)

BECKETT. There's something else.

PINTER. What?

BECKETT. Try as I might, I can't shake off my fear that the man you ran out without facing a ball… was Doggo.

PINTER. Doggo? *(His mind racing.)* Impossible.

BECKETT. Is it?

PINTER. We both *saw* the man I ran out.

BECKETT. Only briefly. Neither of us know who he was. Who's to say he and Doggo aren't one and the same?

*(***PINTER*** tries to process this.)*

You said the man you ran out was our best player. Doggo didn't bowl. So where did he bat?

PINTER. He didn't open. Both the openers played in my first game. I'm pretty sure Doggo didn't.

BECKETT. Paolozzi and Wyse batted three and four.

PINTER. We were five and six.

BECKETT. We know the skipper batted nine.

PINTER. The boy who opened the bowling was number eleven.

BECKETT. Our best player can't have batted at ten. Which means he must have gone in…

PINTER. What's left?

BECKETT. Seven or eight.

PINTER. I don't like where this is going.

BECKETT. Number eight, what was his name?

PINTER. Let me think... Edmund?

BECKETT. Desmond...?

PINTER. Desmond Woolf!

BECKETT. That's it!

PINTER. They call him Wolfie.

BECKETT. How did he bat?

PINTER. He got an inside edge past the keeper for four... Not a convincing shot... Then chipped a harmless half-volley to mid-on.

BECKETT. Hardly our finest player.

PINTER. *(To himself.)* No.

(They both come to the same sober conclusion.)

The truth at last... The man I ran out without facing a ball... the man who was to give us a lift... the man who, you say, cursed me to high heaven and said he never wanted to clap eyes on me again... that man was Doggo.

(A phone rings offstage.)

BECKETT. What's that?

PINTER. A telephone!

BECKETT. Where's it coming from?

*(**PINTER** starts heading over (stage left) to investigate.)*

PINTER. Is that a building of some sort? Hard to make it out against the trees...

BECKETT. There's something odd about this.

PINTER. Yet strangely familiar.

BECKETT. Go. Investigate.

(**PINTER** *goes.* **BECKETT** *starts pacing about.*)

'The one saving grace for the defeated' ...What is it? *una salus victis...* 'is that they have no hope' ...Hope of what? *...nullam sperare... salutem...* 'The one saving grace for the damned...

(**PINTER** *returns.*)

...is that they have no hope of / salvation.'

PINTER. Bad news.

BECKETT. Was it Doggo?

PINTER. He can't come.

BECKETT. Why not?

PINTER. An unexpected plumbing issue.

BECKETT. Him or his aunt?

PINTER. He didn't elaborate. I think he was on the job.

(*Brief pause.* **BECKETT** *thinks.*)

And you won't believe this.

BECKETT. What?

PINTER. We're back at the ground.

BECKETT. Impossible.

PINTER. (*Pointing.*) That building's the pavilion.

BECKETT. How can it be? We didn't take any turns.

PINTER. We must have come in a horseshoe.

The green's right next to the ground. Where we were sitting during the game is just over there.

(**BECKETT** *processes this.*)

BECKETT. My coat!

PINTER. Not there.

BECKETT. What?

PINTER. Someone must have taken it.

> (**BECKETT** *digests the disappointment.*)

BECKETT. Is the pavilion open?

PINTER. No.

BECKETT. Where's the phone?

PINTER. On the outside wall.

> (*The phone rings again. They look at each other.*)

BECKETT. I'll go.

> (**BECKETT** *exits.* **PINTER** *lights a cigarette. Shortly afterwards* **BECKETT** *returns.*)

PINTER. Well?

BECKETT. It seems he's managed to fix it. A defective ballcock. He says to wait. He's coming after all.

> (*They look at each other.*)

PINTER. That's good, isn't it?

BECKETT. I'm not so sure.

PINTER. What do you mean?

BECKETT. First, he said yes, then he said no, now he's saying wait... I think he's toying with us.

> (**BECKETT** *edges downstage.*)

PINTER. You're imagining things.

BECKETT. Am I?

PINTER. I say we wait.

BECKETT. You've said 'wait' before. Look what happened there.

> (**BECKETT** *starts looking out into the distance.*)

PINTER. If you're right, if he is 'toying with us', he'll have to come. Or at least send someone. He'll want to know that we've waited.

BECKETT. *(Peering out.)* What's that?

PINTER. Where?

BECKETT. By the tree.

> (**PINTER** *also peers out.*)

Is that a man?

PINTER. He's wearing a coat.

BECKETT. Is it *him*?

PINTER. It's barely been two minutes.

BECKETT. He's coming towards us.

PINTER. Are you sure?

BECKETT. *(Out towards the man.)* Hello?

PINTER. Why don't you go and check?

BECKETT. You go. *(Quietly.)* Take your bat.

> (**PINTER** *gets his bat and goes downstage and beyond.* **BECKETT** *waits.* **PINTER** *comes back with something.*)

PINTER. It wasn't a man. It was this old thing.

BECKETT. My coat!

PINTER. Draped over a branch.

(**PINTER** *passes the coat.* **BECKETT** *clutches it to him. He takes a moment to reunite with his coat but then returns to his state of unease.*)

BECKETT. How did it get there?

PINTER. Do you think he left it?

BECKETT. Doggo?

PINTER. On his way to his aunt's?

BECKETT. What for?

PINTER. As a sign?

BECKETT. I don't like this.

PINTER. Or a warning…

(*Pause.*)

BECKETT. Let's ring.

PINTER. We don't have his number.

BECKETT. Get it from the operator.

PINTER. He probably won't be there.

BECKETT. His aunt will. Ask if he's left.

(**PINTER** *goes.* **BECKETT** *holds his coat and waits. A phone is heard ringing faintly.* **PINTER** *comes back.*)

PINTER. It didn't work.

BECKETT. What do you mean?

PINTER. I got the number, dialled it, and a phone started ringing somewhere inside the pavilion.

BECKETT. Oh, God!

PINTER. What?

(*He pulls* **PINTER** *close. They whisper initially.*)

BECKETT. He's *here!* He's been here all along.

PINTER. What are you talking about?

BECKETT. He's waiting for us.

PINTER. No, he isn't.

BECKETT. He wants revenge.

PINTER. What about his aunt?

BECKETT. A decoy.

PINTER. Don't be ridiculous.

BECKETT. All I wanted was a quiet weekend. And now I'm about to be done to death by a psychopath.

PINTER. Stop panicking.

BECKETT. In the *fucking* Cotswolds!

PINTER. It's me he wants. If it comes to it, I'll offer myself. Put your coat on, for Christ's sake. Have some whisky.

BECKETT. I can't. My throat's gone numb.

>   (**PINTER** *pours himself a drop more whisky.* **BECKETT** *starts to put on his coat.*)

What's this?

>   (*He finds something jammed into one of the arms.*)

The scorebook!

PINTER. How did it get there?

>   (*They both think. The phone rings.*)

Again?

BECKETT. Answer it!

>   (**PINTER** *goes.* **BECKETT** *tries to read the book by moonlight without success.* **PINTER** *returns.*)

Was it him?

PINTER. He asked if we were comfortable.

BECKETT. *(Agitated.)* Comfortable? *(To himself.)* What's he playing at? *(To* **PINTER.***)* Anything else?

PINTER. He's having trouble starting the car. He's going to try and jump start it from his van. If that doesn't work, he says he'll send a friend.

BECKETT. Another variable to add to the equation…

PINTER. Why not just come in the van?

BECKETT. I don't like it. I think we're being corralled.

Pass the whisky.

> (**PINTER** *gives him the bottle, and lights matches allowing* **BECKETT** *to read the scorebook.*)

Look at this!

PINTER. What?

BECKETT. Someone's filled in the gaps in our innings.

PINTER. Who?

BECKETT. The handwriting's different.

PINTER. Which batsmen?

BECKETT. Seven… and ten.

> *(They look at each other.)*

PINTER. Go on…

BECKETT. Doggo wasn't seven.

PINTER. What?

BECKETT. He was *ten*.

PINTER. Ten? What name did they give him?

BECKETT. *(Looking.)* ... 'Doggo'. No initial.

PINTER. A coincidence?

BECKETT. It can't be. It's part of their revenge.

PINTER. They probably overheard us.

BECKETT. The name's in quotes.

(They look at each other.)

PINTER. So who was seven?

BECKETT. Seven was... Wait...

(Reading with difficulty.) 'Wel-l-ard'.

PINTER. Wellard?

*(**PINTER** fills with horror.)*

Oh God...

Is there an initial?

BECKETT. It's smudged.

PINTER. Not an 'A'?

BECKETT. *(Squinting.)* ...Yes.

How did you know?

PINTER. Arthur Wellard.

BECKETT. I know that name.

Didn't he play for...

PINTER. Somerset.

BECKETT. Of course.

PINTER. And England.

BECKETT. England...

PINTER. Arthur Wellard was one of greatest first-class cricketers of the thirties and forties. They told me he occasionally turned out for these hoodlums. But I didn't believe them.

BECKETT. I vaguely remember him hitting some poor bowler for several consecutive sixes.

PINTER. He still holds the world record for the highest number of runs off a single over in first-class cricket. Thirty. All in sixes. He's probably the greatest six-hitter the game has ever seen.

And I ran him out.

BECKETT. Before he'd faced a ball.

(*The phone rings.* **BECKETT** *motions to rise.*)

PINTER. Don't answer it!

(**BECKETT** *remains still.* **PINTER** *goes to his bag.*)

BECKETT. What are you doing?

PINTER. Padding up.

BECKETT. Padding up?! What for?

PINTER. You should go while you can.

(**PINTER** *gets out his kit and starts putting on his pads.*)

BECKETT. I can't leave you.

PINTER. Go to Adlestrop... Find the station... Sleep in the waiting room... Take the first train to Oxford.

BECKETT. Then what?

PINTER. I don't know. Call my agent. Raise reinforcements.

BECKETT. What about you?

PINTER. I'll stay. And face the music.

BECKETT. Come with me.

PINTER. I'd never make it. Not with this ankle.

> *(They look at each other.)*

Don't worry. I won't go down without a fight.

Not with the fire in me now.

> *(**BECKETT** gets his bag and starts heading off.)*

BECKETT. *(Turning.)* Are you sure?

PINTER. Yes... You go... I'll wait.

> *(Pause. **BECKETT** exits (stage right).)*

> *(As **PINTER** finishes padding up a car is heard entering the pavilion carpark. It stops with the headlights shining on **PINTER**, who braces himself. The car door opens. Someone gets out and closes it. His footsteps are heard, and his shadow is seen approaching from the direction of the pavilion.)*

> *(The man comes to a halt just offstage, his shadow still visible. He is wearing a long coat. **PINTER** stands and moves towards him, keeping his bat at his side.)*

Who's there?

> *(No reply.)*

Answer me!

> *(No reply. **PINTER** takes a step forward, his bat still concealed, and peers at the silhouetted figure again...)*

Sam?

Blackout

Epilogue

(Dawn, Adlestrop station. No birdsong. **PINTER**, *using his bag as a pillow, is asleep on a platform bench with 'ADLESTROP' written above him. Enter* **BECKETT** *(stage right) with bag. He walks up to the platform edge, looks both ways, approaches* **PINTER** *quietly, and leans over.)*

BECKETT. *(Like a cricket call.)* Wait!

PINTER. Aagghh!

(Gathering his wits.) Sam?

BECKETT. You made it.

PINTER. So it seems.

*(**PINTER** slowly tries to get from a lying position to a standing one without sitting (due to a back pain).)*

BECKETT. When did you get here?

PINTER. No idea. My watch is broken.

BECKETT. I'll get mine.

*(**BECKETT** starts rummaging through his bag.)*

So they came?

*(**PINTER** is focused on getting to his feet.)*

And brought you straight here?

*(**BECKETT** finds his watch and looks at it.)*

It's stopped.

*(**PINTER** finally gets to a standing position.)*

Is there a train?

PINTER. There's a timetable.

BECKETT. You've looked?

PINTER. There are unresolved issues.

BECKETT. Care to enumerate?

PINTER. One, there's a drip down the column for Adlestrop, rendering it illegible.

> (**BECKETT** *heads over to the timetable and briefly scans it.*)

Two, even if we guess when the first train is, we don't have a working watch.

Three, we don't know if the timetable is current or whether the station – or line – is still in use.

BECKETT. I did check my watch a couple of minutes ago. When it was working.

PINTER. What time was it then?

BECKETT. *(Straining to remember.)* … It's gone.

PINTER. What does it say now?

BECKETT. *(Looking.)* Five thirty-six.

If I wind it up and move it two minutes forward, that should get us within.. two minutes of the correct time.

> (**PINTER** *grapples with the logic of this.* **BECKETT** *winds up his watch.*)

There's a train every half hour… Assuming we're roughly halfway between the stations either side of here, that should be… between thirty-eight and forty past… Factoring in the watch's margin of error, that's somewhere between… thirty-six and forty-two past… It's now… five thirty-eight, so we need to wait… *four* minutes to find out if there are trains.

PINTER. *(Totally confused.)* Right.

(**PINTER** *takes out his bottle of whisky and has a swig.* **BECKETT** *looks at him askance.*)

(*Matter of fact.*) It's been topped up.

BECKETT. How?

PINTER. I've no idea.

(**PINTER** *motions to put the bottle away.*)

BECKETT. May I?

PINTER. I thought you didn't drink before five.

BECKETT. I'm still regarding this as yesterday.

(**PINTER** *passes the bottle and ponders the metaphysics of this remark.* **BECKETT** *sits, has a gulp, and returns the bottle.* **PINTER** *remains standing.*)

Can you not sit?

PINTER. No. My back.

(*Beat.*)

BECKETT. Was it them?

(*No reply.* **PINTER** *moves gingerly to the platform edge and looks one way then the other.*)

PINTER. Where's this train coming from?

BECKETT. I haven't the foggiest.

(*They wait in silence for a while.*)

PINTER. So… do you think you might play for us again?

BECKETT. Let's see… I've cracked my skull… been run out needlessly… was terrorised by unseen malign forces… and am now marooned miles from civilisation.

Probably not. If I'm brutally honest.

PINTER. Next week we're at Sidcup...

BECKETT. No offence.

It's not personal.

PINTER. I didn't take it personally.

BECKETT. At least, not *meant* as personal.

> (*Awkward pause.*)

I could come and watch on the odd occasion.

> (**PINTER** *absorbs the apparent concession.*)

It'll provide an opportunity for *schadenfreude*, if nothing else.

> (*Beat.*)

What was it Lucretius said?

PINTER. (*Half to himself.*) Rrrhh...

BECKETT. *suave... e terra magnum alterius spectare laborem.*

> (*Again, there is the rigmarole of* **PINTER** *looking blank.*)

'Sweet it is to look, from a safe distance, upon the travails of others.'

> (*Pause.* **PINTER** *turns and heads downstage. He looks left for ten seconds.*)

PINTER. Time?

BECKETT. (*Checking.*) Five-forty-two and fifty seconds.

> (**PINTER** *looks right for ten seconds.*)

PINTER. That's it. No trains.

>(**PINTER** *tries to sit but cannot and so tries to lie again. Soon after, the sound of an approaching train is heard (from the right). As* **PINTER** *struggles to his feet, the train passes without slowing. They watch in silence.)*

BECKETT. None that stop...

>*(Pause.* **PINTER** *sighs, worn out by variously getting up and lying down.)*

PINTER. *(Offering the bottle.)* Drink?

BECKETT. No.

>*(***BECKETT** *starts pacing about with a sense of disquiet.)*

PINTER. What now?

BECKETT. What if we just headed off? Alongside the tracks.

PINTER. To where?

BECKETT. Wherever they lead.

>*(They get their bags but* **PINTER** *heads left,* **BECKETT** *right. They pause and look back at each other.)*

PINTER. Is it that way?

BECKETT. The same way as the train...

PINTER. What if it was coming *from* Oxford?

BECKETT. *(Digesting this.)* I still think this way.

PINTER. Deeper into the Cotswolds?

BECKETT. We'd soon come out the other side.

>*(Beat.)*

PINTER. If it did come from Oxford, there must be trains going back. They can't all be piling up in the arse of nowhere.

> (**BECKETT** *seems less certain.*)

BECKETT. Maybe it *is* the other platform.

> (**BECKETT** *walks downstage and peers across.*)

There doesn't seem to be a timetable on that side…

> (**PINTER** *heads over to the timetable on this platform. He bends down with a wince, and notices something.*)

PINTER. For Christ's sake!

BECKETT. What?

PINTER. It's here.

BECKETT. Where?

PINTER. Below the first.

BECKETT. How did we miss it?

PINTER. *(Sheepish.)* It's quite far down.

BECKETT. What does it say?

PINTER. *(Trying.)* I can't get low enough.

BECKETT. *(To himself.)* Every man has his specialty.

> (**BECKETT** *goes over, kneels and reads.*)

I don't believe it!

PINTER. What?

BECKETT. The column we need is illegible again.

PINTER. The same drip?

BECKETT. *(Frustrated.)* Eli, eli lama sabakthani!

PINTER. What the hell is that?

BECKETT. Hebrew. Christ's last words to his father.

> (**PINTER** *looks contrite about not recognising it.* **BECKETT** *gets up, regathers, and looks both ways.*)

There's still a chance there'll be a train to Oxford on *that* platform.

> (*No reaction.*)

I'm going across.

> (**BECKETT** *exits (right) with bag.* **PINTER** *waits momentarily then follows. Soon* **BECKETT** *enters the auditorium (the other platform) and sits.* **PINTER** *enters shortly afterwards and goes over to* **BECKETT**. *He tries tentatively to recline on the floor. There is the faint noise of a train.*)

PINTER. Agh, my back!

BECKETT. Shh! (*Looking stage left.*) I can hear a train.

> (**BECKETT** *tries to concentrate.*)

PINTER. (*Focusing.*) Is it slowing down?

BECKETT. Possibly.

> (*A train pulls up...*)

Jesus wept! It's the other platform!

PINTER. Go! Take it!

> (**BECKETT** *grabs his bag and exits hastily,* **PINTER** *rises with difficulty and does likewise a few seconds behind. As* **BECKETT** *reappears on the other platform, a whistle blows.*)

BECKETT. *(To* **PINTER** *still offstage.)* Come on!

> *(***BECKETT*** waits. The train goes. Enter* **PINTER.***)*

PINTER. You should have gone.

BECKETT. I couldn't.

> *(They take some time to absorb the disappointment.* **BECKETT** *sits. Suddenly the platform phone rings.)*

PINTER. What's that?

BECKETT. A telephone.

PINTER. Not again.

BECKETT. Answer it!

PINTER. *(Sitting.)* I can't. I'm shattered.

> *(***BECKETT*** gets up and answers it.)*

BECKETT. Hello... Who? ... The stationmaster?... *(Looking around.)* There isn't one... There's no one else here... What?... We were playing cricket nearby... Yesterday... Who am I?

(To **PINTER.***)* Who shall I say I am?

> *(***PINTER*** shrugs his shoulders.* **BECKETT** *has a sudden thought.)*

I'm the Serjeant Surgeon to her Majesty the Queen.

> *(***PINTER*** looks at* **BECKETT** *in bemusement.)*

Her senior doctor... It's a post going back to Edward the Third... I'm not making it up... It's in *Debrett's*... Serjeant with a 'j' ... My name?

(To **PINTER.***)* What's the Queen's doctor called?

PINTER. How should I know?

(*Suddenly.*) Wait, I've actually met him. He was at press night of *The Caretaker*... 'Lord' something... Wait... (*Racking his brains.*) Porritt! That's it.

BECKETT. (*To the phone.*) Hello?... Sorry... The name's Porritt... *Lord* Porritt... What?... Of course we have... They don't seem to stop... The thing is, I need to get back to London at once... I'm due to operate today... Not the queen... (*Aside.*) Eejit!... (*To the phone again.*) Her great aunt... It's extremely delicate... Fortunately, my area of specialisation... Where?... The anorectal junction... Oh, I see... St Mary's, Paddington... Is there any way you could arrange a lift?... For the both of us... The other is my anaesthetist... Unfortunately, he was playing as well... He's the only man I trust with this particular procedure.

(*Listening for a while.*) You can?... That's marvellous!... Her Majesty will be hugely relieved... As will her great aunt.

(**BECKETT** *makes a positive gesture to* **PINTER**.)

(*To the phone.*) A mainline station would be tremendous!... And that's by car...? (*Listening for a while.*) Oh... I see... Of course not. We're very grateful... Should we head to the... Right... By the station? ...Yes, that's... No... We'll wait.

(**BECKETT** *puts the phone down.*)

PINTER. Well?

BECKETT. He can get us to Banbury. By horse.

PINTER. Horse?

BECKETT. A local farmer is going to get us horses and ride with us to Banbury. From there we can get the mainline train to Marylebone. He's coming over right away. The stables are close.

PINTER. I've never ridden a horse.

(**BECKETT** *sighs.*)

BECKETT. We could always stay here. Waiting…

(*Beat.*)

PINTER. No. Let's ride.

BECKETT. Will you be able to get on?

PINTER. With my ankle?

BECKETT. With your back.

PINTER. I'll manage.

(*They both take a moment to absorb the seemingly resolved situation.*)

BECKETT. I think I might rest a moment. At least until we hear the clop of hooves.

(**BECKETT** *reclines. Almost straightaway we hear the sound of hooves (offstage).*)

PINTER. He's here. That was quick.

BECKETT. (*Stirring.*) You go ahead. Check that you can mount your steed. I need to use the little boys' room.

(**PINTER** *exits with bag (right).* **BECKETT** *gets up and goes off to relieve himself (left). Meanwhile a train arrives on the original platform. The train duly leaves. Soon after* **PINTER** *re-enters with his bag, huffing.*)

PINTER. There's no way I can get on a horse.

(*He scans platform.*)

Sam?

(He gazes at the train as it fades out of view and earshot.)

'One man left and one man came on the bare platform'.

*(**PINTER** turns and goes to the bench. He lies down as at the start of the scene. He swiftly falls asleep. After a pause, we start to hear the sound of birdsong. Soon after **BECKETT** enters with his bag (right), as at the start of the scene. He walks along the platform and notices the sleeping **PINTER**. He walks back to the noticeboard and peruses it. He returns to **PINTER** and stands over him. He gently lowers his bag.)*

BECKETT. *(Like a cricket call.)* Wait!

PINTER. Aagghh!

(Gathering his wits.) Sam!

*(He puts his hand on **BECKETT**'s arm to make sure he is really there.)*

Am I glad to see you.

BECKETT. You look like you've seen a ghost?

*(No reply. They both sit quietly for a moment. **PINTER** gets his bag. As he does so, he notices something.)*

PINTER. Listen.

BECKETT. What?

PINTER. They're back.

BECKETT. Who?

PINTER. The birds...

BECKETT. ...Of Oxfordshire and Gloucestershire.

(As they take a moment to listen to the birdsong, we hear the faint sound of horses whinnying nearby.)

PINTER. What was that?

BECKETT. There's a man out front with horses.

PINTER. What?

BECKETT. He looked vaguely familiar.

*(**PINTER** looks uneasy. The phone rings.)*

I'll get it.

(He heads to the phone but then stops and turns...)

Yes?

(Half a beat.)

PINTER. No!

(The phone keeps ringing, the sound getting louder...)

Blackout

ABOUT THE AUTHOR

Shomit Dutta is a playwright, translator, teacher and amateur cricketer.

Stumped, his first play to be produced professionally, has its first production in Bath, Cambridge and London and a second production shortly afterwards in Dublin. His earlier works include *Changing of the Guard*, performed at the O' Reilly Theatre in 2016 and a version of *Aristophanes' Birds* performed at the Oxford Playhouse in 2000. He is currently developing two more plays, one about two Second-World-War magicians and the other about an encounter between Oscar Wilde and Walt Whitman. He is also working on a play about the baroque painter Artemisia Gentileschi.

Shomit has had three volumes of Greek tragedy published: Sophocles' *Ajax* (Cambridge University Press 2001); Aeschylus' *Agamemnon*, Sophocles' *Oedipus*, Euripides' *Medea* and selections from Aristophanes' *Frogs* and Aristotle's *Poetics* (Penguin 2004); and Aristophanes' *Wasps, Women at the Thesmophoria* and *Frogs* (Penguin 2007).

While completing a D Phil on ancient Greek comedy and tragedy he taught at Oxford and Cork Universities. He has also taught Latin and Greek for many years at several schools.

He also writes book reviews – mainly fiction and books on the classical world and cricket – and articles for newspapers and journals, including *The Guardian*, *The Observer*, *The Telegraph*, *The Times Literary Supplemen*t, *The New Statesman* and *The Nightwatchman* (a.k.a. *The Wisden Cricket Quarterly*).

Shomit has been playing cricket all his life, and has been an avid member of Gaieties Cricket Club for over twenty years.

Ingram Content Group UK Ltd.
Milton Keynes UK
UKHW021255020623
422777UK00016B/120

9 780573 013645